Watching My Wife Die

A TRUE STORY

A Christian's Perspective On Grieving

DONALD L. GILLELAND

Copyright © 2020 by Donald L. Gilleland.

ISBN   Softcover   978-1-953537-22-5

All rights reserved. No part of this book may be reproduced or transmitted in any form or by any means, electronic or mechanical, including photocopying, recording, or by any information storage and retrieval system without express written permission from the author, except in the case of brief quotations embodied in critical reviews and certain other non-commercial uses permitted by copyright law.

Printed in the United States of America.

To order additional copies of this book, contact:
Bookwhip
1-855-339-3589
https://www.bookwhip.com

CONTENTS

Preface v

Chapter 1. The Origin of This Book 1

Chapter 2. The Stages of Grief 12

Chapter 3. Stage One—Denial and Isolation 18

Chapter 4. Stage Two—Anger 26

Chapter 5. Stage Three—Bargaining 32

Chapter 6. Stage Four—Depression 37

Chapter 7. Stage Five—Acceptance 42

Chapter 8. Other Possible Stages of Grief 48

Conclusions 51

Editor's Note 61

PREFACE

On December 28, 2018 I lost the love of my life. After being together for 62 years (two years dating and 60 years married), our Lord took my wife, Margaret (Peggy) Gilleland, home to spend eternity with Him in heaven. In my wildest imagination I did not expect the pain of her loss to be so great. It is absolutely devastating at a pronounced depth that shocked me to my core.

Peggy wasn't just the love of my life; she was and still is the central focus of my life. She is the person I shared all my dreams with, all of my anxieties and joys with. She was the foundation of my very existence, and now she is gone, and I have to reconcile her death with the fact that I may live another eight or ten years without her. That is a thought that scares me to death, because she was the core of my existence.

Incidentally, she hated the name Margaret and insisted her entire life that she be called Peggy. She never tried to explain why she hated Margaret; she just insisted that she be called Peggy.

I should have known that her absence from my life would be unbearable. We spent so much time together doing everything as a couple that I never in my wildest imaginations gave any thought to what my life would be like without her, particularly as I will explain later, since she and I both thought I would be the first to die.

Peggy has been gone over 18 months, yet it still seems as if she died yesterday. I see her or feel her presence almost everywhere, especially in every room of our house. That is understandable because, except for periods when I served in isolated or remote assignments in the military, we literally did almost everything together throughout those 62 years, and now it is unbearable for me to walk through our empty house. There are glaring reminders of her presence in every single room, almost on every wall.

It sometimes feels like her loss is some sort of punishment God has laid on me; as though I have done something wrong, and now I must endure such strong and complicated emotions, unlike any I have ever experienced during my 84 years on Earth, as a form of retribution. On first blush, the pain of losing Peggy is beyond anything I could ever have imagined, because neither of us ever thought she would be the first to go. In a matter of days after her death, I became aware of a huge hole in my heart that will never be full again.

Intellectually I know God didn't take Peggy as a form of punishment for me. That would be illogical. No loving God would be so vengeful! He doesn't do such spiteful things, even to people who might deserve it. Nevertheless, it is almost impossible to fathom why He would take her from me to be with Him, when He knows how much we love each other. God isn't the only one who knows that. Everyone who knows us knows how much we love each other.

I know He didn't take her to punish me, but it sometimes feels like a form of punishment. I know He loves me and cares about my welfare, but it still feels like a form of chastisement. Sometimes I just get caught up in my own ego issues that trample all over God's sovereignty. I yell at Him and tell him how disappointed I am in Him, and ask Him why he has done this to me, why He has left me alone to live without Peggy in some kind of a new normal that I don't even recognize.

Establishing a new normal, while living without her, will require a herculean effort over a long period of time. She was an unbelievably gifted, talented and caring woman who I was fortunate enough to live with most of my life. But this new normal is only the tip of an iceberg that involves an inconceivable amount and variety of pain. This book is about dying and grief and how my wife and I reacted to them.

I don't pretend to be an authority on this topic, and I have no medical background. But I am an authority on how much my wife suffered over a long period of time and how her death caused an extended period of grief for me. This book is about how we handled these two issues over a nearly two-year period.

First, I will cover Peggy's 18-month struggle with ovarian cancer, including how she never once complained about it, then I will spend some time explaining how I reacted to her death and how much I was and continue to be affected by grief. Grieving over my wife's death is unlike anything else I have ever experienced. I grieved when my mother died many years ago, but it was modest contrasted with the grief I feel now over the death of my wonderful wife.

To understand her struggle with ovarian cancer and my struggle with grief, I must first tell you a bit about our relationship early in our lives, as well as over this difficult period. It's almost impossible to fill in the blanks on a long marriage with just a few words or sentences, so I will take some time to make sure you understand what a spectacular wife she was and what a sensational, loving and God centered life we shared together.

Our story began in 1956 while we were attending Southern Illinois University, but I'll get to that later. For now, I'll start by telling you a little bit about both of us and about our extraordinary love affair.

CHAPTER ONE

The Origin of This Book

To begin, I am not a doctor, or counselor, or anything remotely like that. I am a writer who doesn't have a specialty. During the past 30 years I have had more than 700 major Op-Ed articles featured in newspapers and magazines literally around the world, including publications in England, France, the Republic of the Philippines, Sweden, the United Arab Emirates, and several island nations; and, of course, the United States.

I write about any topic that pricks my interest. I do the research necessary to cover a topic that interests me, and then I write about that topic. I have also written six books, four on various aspects of America, one on my wife's struggle with metastatic ovarian cancer and a memoir.

I am in love with my country, which is why I have written so much about America. I am convinced that God has blessed our country with attributes that set us apart from the rest of the world and make it possible for us to hold out hope for the 21st Century.

All of my books are listed on Amazon.com/books. If you type in my name, all of my books will come up, along with a great many book reviews by people I don't even know. Fortunately, they are all mostly very good reviews, five points out of a possible five points.

While it may seem strange, I find that some people never suspect that it takes a lot longer to do the research than it does to write an article or a book. Even when you know a topic well, there are a myriad of things you take for granted and need to research to flesh out an in depth article or a book.

What brought me to the topic of grieving was my wife's battle with metastatic ovarian cancer. She was an incredibly gifted woman who loved to whiz through crossword puzzles that I wouldn't even try. She was an even more incredibly gifted Christian who loved to participate in church programs and who studied the Bible like a graduate student wanting to absorb everything she can about the topic.

More than that, she was a lovable woman who projected a caring attitude about helping other people. As you might guess, I adored this woman for 62 years. In fact, I still adore her and probably will for whatever time I have left on this Earth. She is the only woman I have ever loved, and is probably the only woman I will ever love.

It may sound a bit like Pollyanna, but living with Peggy was at once unimaginably exciting, yet very comforting. It was a joy to wake up every morning knowing that this magnificent woman loved me as much as I loved her.

Those years with Peggy were more satisfying, fulfilling, and ecstatic than I ever expected them to be. Like most marriages, we had severe problems in the early years of our marriage adjusting to each other. We were like oil and water. She was a vibrant extrovert and I was a bit of an introvert. We were both fascinated with each other's personality, but were sometimes surprised by facets that we didn't expect.

However, even the difficult years when we first married proved to be wonderful because, as most of you know, making up after a difficult period can be spectacular. And making up with Peggy was beyond spectacular!

The first 10 or 12 years were wonderful, exciting, and awful, all at the same time. They were wonderful because we were so much in love, but they were awful because God wasn't the focus of our marriage. However, the last 50 years with God at the center of our marriage were extraordinary. I discovered that Peggy was a remarkable gift from God.

From the very first day I met Peggy at Southern Illinois University in 1956, I have never ever wanted, or been interested in, any other woman. Peggy fulfilled all my dreams. She was beautiful, vivacious, and a great life partner. She fascinated me throughout the more than 22,000 days we shared together, even the early days while we were getting to know each other.

By almost any measure, Peggy was more than I ever dreamed of having in a wife. She loved me every bit as much as I loved her and she made sure I felt that love, right up to the day she died. She also had a wonderful sense of humor right up to the end. When the van for the Palm Bay, Florida Hospice Center came to pick her up to take her to its Palm Bay facility, the driver could tell that she was too weak to get out of her chair, so he asked her if he could pick her up. She said "of course." When he bent down to pick her up she looked up at him and said, "what a brute."

That was all the more poignant because it was during the last stage of her life. She would die within the next 28 hours, keeping her sense of humor to the end.

But that was not something new. She had a rich sense of humor throughout our marriage and into the final stages of her life. For instance, when the doctor told us she had ovarian cancer, she quickly retorted: "I can't have, I've never used them," highlighting the fact that we never had any children. I'll touch on that a bit later.

Once Peggy was comfortably placed in the van, the driver suggested that I wait an hour to follow so that the Hospice Center could get her settled. When I walked into the Hospice Center, I found that she had already been given morphine and a sedative, and she looked sleepy, but comfortable.

When I walked over to her bed she immediately reached up, grabbed my hand, and squeezed it firmly. I bent down to give her a kiss and she reached up to put her arms around my neck. "I love you," she said. "I love you too honey," I said. At that point she passed out and never woke up again. She had deliberately struggled to stay alert long enough to say goodbye to me. Those were our very last words. And what wonderful words they were! I can't imagine a better end time memory, but I have a lifetime of extraordinary memories of my sweet, wonderful wife.

Peggy and I had something very special throughout our marriage, and almost anyone who knew us could tell you about it.

Our first date was epic, because it was at once exciting, yet a bit sad. It was exciting because being with Peggy was the thrill of a lifetime. It was kind of sad because I dumped another date unceremoniously to be with Peggy. I always felt badly about the way I treated that other date, but I was absolutely sure Peggy and I had started something that was going to be magical. And I was right. 62 years of magical.

Even today I get excited just thinking about the years we spent together. Peggy was a thrill a minute for me and loving her was truly magical.

Over the years we lived in 12 states and travelled the world together. Wherever we went her personality attracted potential friends like a magnet. Everybody loved Peggy. I adored her right from the first time we met, which was itself a bit unusual.

We were both communication majors at Southern Illinois University (SIU), with a principal focus on the theater. We both loved acting. In fact, I had planned to become a professional actor, and worked on every SIU theatrical play during my four undergraduate years. I also had worked in two seasons of summer stock and travelled with a touring theater for three months. But I hadn't planned on falling in love.

I first met Peggy on stage. SIU was then on a quarter system. She started school in the Fall and I started in the Winter, so the Theater Department had already put on one play. When I first walked on stage, the players were "striking" the set, taking it apart to get ready for the next show.

I saw two sets of feet sticking out from underneath the scenery. One set belonged to Peggy and the other belonged to her steady boyfriend. We met when they climbed out from under the set. I was immediately captivated by the way she looked and by her humor. The first thing she said to me was, "Are you just studying the set or are you going to help us?" I helped them and loved watching her.

Her boyfriend subsequently became my college roommate. That was just serendipitous, not planned. I didn't even know the guy. He just happened to come with the room I rented. He ultimately resigned from school after failing freshman English three times.

For a time, I admired Peggy from a distance, all the while wishing I could date her. I was instantly attracted to her vivacious personality that was dramatically different than mine. She was imaginative, flighty and full of energy. Everyone in the theater department seemed to know and love her.

One day her boyfriend came home in a huff and said they had broken up over something; I don't remember what it was. I told him, "if you're not going to date her I'm going to see if she will go out with me."

I asked her out and she said yes. That was the end of him and the beginning of us. We dated throughout the rest of our time in college, marrying during our senior year. That too was a mark of Peggy's adaptability. When we married we had a two-bedroom apartment, with a hide-away kitchen covered by a drawstring.

Our apartment was located above a movie theater, which we thought might be loud, but we never heard a peek from it. We had practically no furniture, but Peggy never once complained. She was satisfied with makeshift bookcases made out of 1"x6" boards stretched between two stacks of bricks, and she served dinners on our ironing board (we didn't have a table). Our furniture remained meager throughout my senior year.

She cooked on a two-burner stove. At first she didn't even know how to boil water. She once boiled a chicken and didn't know the stuffing was on the inside of the bird. She also once baked a pumpkin pie, but didn't put any sugar in it. Nevertheless, over the years she became a sensational cook, and we had frequent dinner parties, and friends would marvel at her ingenuity and artistry.

She was so desperate to make our marriage succeed on the modest amount of money I made working part time for the theater department that she quit school and went to work in the local hospital as a nurse's aide, while I finished my senior year. I had a lot of trouble with that. I hated that as a 110-pound woman she often had to lift very heavy old men. But, again, she never complained.

Our early marriage was exciting, but it was a bumpy road for about 10 years until we decided to put Jesus Christ in the center of it. After that, our marriage became the most fascinating and successful thing we ever tried together.

We found something to love about everywhere we ever lived all 12 states and several countries; but by far our happiest times were the 26 years we spent in Florida, after I retired from General Dynamics Corporation.

We both hated cold weather and snow, so as I approached retirement, Peggy said to me: "when you retire we're going to live somewhere we never have to worry about winter or snow." To make that happen, I used all my vacation time for three years doing site surveys, trying to find the perfect place to retire. Peggy loved checking out cities as potential retirement sites.

We went to North and South Carolina, Alabama, Georgia, and Florida. We would visit a site in the summer and return in the winter. Even though we loved the summers in lots of cities, we hated their winters. So we continued south until we fell in love with Melbourne, Florida. To be more precise, we fell in love with an unincorporated section, just north of Melbourne, called Suntree. It fit the bill perfectly. It was beautiful and had wonderful year-round weather.

It also had two 18-hole, championship golf courses that hosted the seniors' tour every year. We joined the golf club and played a lot of golf on both courses after retirement. Peggy was a dichotomy. She could knock the cover off the golf ball from the tee, but couldn't putt. We both enjoyed playing with each other. But I digress.

Following college, Peggy worked in a variety of administrative positions while I completed my military career. I had previously served enlisted in the Navy for eight years before graduating from college and subsequently finished up 22 years in the Air Force, retiring as a Lieutenant Colonel. I had served in all but two ranks from Seaman Recruit to Lieutenant Colonel.

After retirement from the Air Force, I worked ten years in the defense industry, retiring from General Dynamics Corporation as its corporate director of public affairs, responsible for worldwide news media relations.

She worked for the U.S. Army as an administrative assistant and a management analysis until 1981 when she decided to stay home and do volunteer work in our community.

Peggy was a gifted mimic, able to speak in almost any dialect, which was a great asset for an actress, which was her initial goal when she entered SIU. She hadn't intended to fall in love either, but we had a strong romantic attraction for each other right from the start.

Over the years she retained her love for reading, particularly reading aloud, as she had done when she studied theater. Later, when we moved to Florida, she was a reader for the Brevard Association for the Advancement of the Blind (BAAB), located in Satellite Beach, Florida, where she recorded books and other literature for a Library of Congress program in which blind people check out and listen to literary works they would not otherwise be able to read.

She often brought creative interpretations to her readings, changing her voice to create characters. She was so good at it that folks occasionally would write letters to let the BAAB leadership know how much they enjoyed her readings.

In fact, her readings are shelved in libraries all over the United States, even today. Her theatre background was evident in her readings because, by a variety of ways, she could assume the identity of each character.

Even more important, she was a dedicated Christian and a volunteer at Calvary Chapel Viera, a branch of Calvary Chapel Melbourne, in West Melbourne, Florida. Calvary Chapel Viera is where we attended church, and where she ran the Information Center for eight years. I continue to attend church there.

She worked in a circular information center at the entrance to the church and anyone who wanted to know anything about our church would stop by her information center where they would find she had an unbelievable font of knowledge about our church. Over the course of eight years working that center she made an amazing number of close friends, many of who later came to her memorial service.

Peggy also regularly attended bible study classes too, because she was happiest when she was working for our Lord or helping other people. Jesus Christ was Peggy's primary focus in life. She literally spent two or three hours every single day studying the bible. I suspect that few people know what a biblical scholar she really was. I will never ever know the bible the way Peggy knew it.

We went to Israel with Pastor Mark Balmer, the main pastor at Calvary Chapel Melbourne, once in 2004 and again in 2007. They were watershed years for us, as we reconfirmed that Jesus Christ was at the center of our marriage. In 2004 Peggy was even baptized again in the center of the Jordan River. She was happiest when Jesus Christ was the visible head of our household.

Peggy had a unique gift that enabled her to make other people laugh, bringing joy to everyone around her. She was an extraordinary mimic who made interesting interpretations of her theater readings, but she was also an awesome comic even without mimicry. Those who knew her recognized her talents immediately.

Right to the very end Peggy enjoyed reading the Bible every day and reading for the Brevard Association for the Advancement of the Blind. She was proud of the fact that she could help people who had trouble with their eyesight.

It is particularly fitting that Peggy, who inspired me, kept me on a level plane, and made me laugh as no one else ever could, has gone to meet our Lord, paving a way for me to follow her to heaven. And I trust that her path to heaven will work for me too, because biblical scripture gives us all real hope of one day being reunited with our loved ones who preceded us to heaven.

I believe one part of the Bible is greatly misunderstood. It is the part that says, "At the resurrection people will neither marry nor be given in marriage; they will be like the angels in heaven" (Matthew 22:30). This is where I believe there is a great misunderstanding. Notice it does not say married folks who enter heaven will no longer be married. Rather it says, "…people will neither marry nor be given in marriage."

It is my opinion that means if you are single when you enter heaven, you will never marry in heaven. That is because in heaven reproduction will not be necessary and therefore there will be no need to be married. However, it doesn't mean that folks who arrive in heaven already married will cease to be married in heaven. I believe Peggy and I will continue to be married throughout eternity, and, even now, I continue to wear my wedding ring.

Notice the bible says that we will be reunited with our family and loved ones. If you think that through, how can there be families without mothers and fathers, ergo there will be married couples in heaven. The bible says nothing about divorcing married couples when they reach heaven. I am convinced that Peggy and I will be reunited in heaven as a married couple to spend all of eternity with each other and God.

To those of you reading this who loved her, I say cherish her memory because you are not likely to find another Peggy in your lifetime. I know I won't! I have not only lost my wife, I've lost my best friend and soul mate.

I have absolutely no doubt that Peggy is happy in heaven, with a new, healthy body. That is important because cancer and chemotherapy caused her to lose 80 pounds before she died, leaving her with just a shell of her former self. While I miss her terribly, I am thankful that she is in heaven with a whole, new body.

All I can ask of God is that He not wait too long to call me home to be with her. I only hope that when the time comes, I am as ready as she was to meet our Lord. She had absolutely no fear of death and was eager to meet Jesus Christ as well as her other family members. Her only regret was that she did not want to leave me, but she was ready for heaven.

In fact, I found out after she died that she told several of her friends that, "while she really hated to leave me, she was extremely tired and ready for heaven." She also asked them to look after me when she was gone because she said, "He's going to be a basket case." And she was right! She knew me well!

I know that some people get mad at God when he takes away a loved one. I have no issue with God, because He gave me so many wonderful years with Peggy. From my perspective, everybody ought to have a Peggy in his or her life, and I will be forever grateful to God for putting her in my life. Everyone should be so blessed!

For sure, even as I write these words, Peggy has already been in heaven for more than seven months. Perhaps what I've written in this book will give you some idea of why my grief over her death is so profound, despite knowing where she is and that I will one day be reunited with her for eternity.

As Colin Smith, senior pastor of The Orchard Evangelical Free Church in Chicago points out in "Will We know Each Other in Heaven," in **Unlocking the Bible**, will we know each other in heaven? Let's cut to the chase with a one-word answer: 'yes!' The two-word answer would be, 'For sure!' And the five-word answer would be, 'You can count on it!'" He then offers seven biblical passages that he believes point to our knowing one another in the resurrection, and some of them point to believers knowing one another immediately after death.

Meanwhile, it will be a daily struggle for me to get through any kind of existence without my wonderful wife and partner in life. I have no idea how long it will take to recover from the severe pain I feel as I try to adjust to the kind of grief I have never experienced, which is ever- present now and leaves me physically and emotionally exhausted. I know it will take a while to write this book, so my perspective on these events may change a bit even as I am writing.

I am mindful of a hopeful Bible passage, Psalm 25:16-17, "Turn to me and be gracious to me, for I am lonely and afflicted. The troubles of my heart have multiplied; free me from my anguish."

I have talked to several friends who lost loved ones and asked them how long it took to get thorough their grief. Every one of them said they will grieve forever, but the worst part took varying amounts of time for them, from about one to two years. I'm sure my grief won't be much different than that, and I don't look forward to such a long sad period.

Going through predictable affects of grief, including shock, frustration, disappointment, isolation, eating irregularly, difficulty concentrating, difficulty remembering things, as well as perpetual headaches and an upset stomach, are common physical and emotional reactions to grief.

Even so, knowing what I might feel during those two years won't take the pain away, but it helps to know that eventually a lot of the pain will leave, and I may return to a semblance of normality. Another biblical passage is relevant: "He heals the brokenhearted and binds up their wounds" (Psalm 147.3).

Shortly after Peggy died, I started attending a 15-week church course titled Grief Share in which the process and various stages of grief were covered in a weekly television series, followed by detailed discussions by the members of our class. What was particularly welcome was seeing that all 14 or 15 members (varied weekly) expressed their pain in a variety of ways. As it turned out each of us was going through stages that were similar for all of us.

Friends frequently asked me if I'm eating regularly and well. Neighbors and friends brought over a lot of meals to make sure I was well taken care of. It seems as if everyone I know wants to take me out to dinner. I finally had to explain to them how much I appreciated all of their efforts, but I need some time alone occasionally.

While I enjoy their support, coming from all directions as it has was at times overwhelming. From time to time I need to be alone just to recharge my batteries. Fortunately they seemed to understand that, once I explained it to them in gentle terms.

CHAPTER TWO

The Stages of Grief

Almost everyone I've ever heard speak about grief and all the books I've read about grief state very clearly that grief is different for everyone and there is no clear path to deal with it. Some say there are five stages of grief, while others claim there are more. But what they all seem to agree on is this: grief is a normal, natural, and a necessary process for healing.

Don't be misled by stoic people who think that grieving is a show of weakness. Nothing could be further from the truth. There is evidence that trying to ignore or avoid grief won't work. It will only make the process of grieving last longer and maybe even cause more pain.

Being independent is generally thought to be the purview of strong people who don't rely on others to accomplish life goals. However, when it comes to grieving, being strong doesn't mean being unemotional, stoic, or pretending it doesn't hurt. Quite the contrary, letting yourself grieve and seeking help to deal with grief may be the strongest thing you can do when you've lost the most important person in your life.

From my perspective there is nothing quite the equivalent of realizing that you will never see your loved one again in this lifetime. It is the most painful thing I have ever experienced, and I have no idea how long it will be before I quit hurting. Losing my wife was and is the most painful thing I have ever experienced.

Elisabeth Kubler-Ross in her 1969 book *On Death and Dying*, wrote that there are five stages of grief. In fact Julie Axelrod, who writes for **Psych Central**, agreed and wrote a book titled **The 5 Stages of Grief and Loss.** She identified the stages as: 1. Denial and Isolation; 2. Anger; 3. Bargaining; 4. Depression; and 5. Acceptance.

Of course, since grief is different for everyone, and while most people will probably go through all five stages, they may not go through them sequentially. The truth is that some people may not even go through all of them, and still others may go thorough more than one at the same time.

David Kessler, who co-authored two books with the legendary Elisabeth Kubler-Ross, adapted her well-respected stages of dying for those in grief. In one of their books **On Grief and Grieving**, they explain how the stages have evolved since their original introduction. Kessler points out the stages of grieving were never meant to help tuck messy emotions into neat packages. "They are responses to loss that many people have, but there is not a typical response to loss as there is no typical loss."

The various stages of grief tend to be merely guides in the grieving process. Some people experience grief by crying, which I often do because I don't seem to have much control over the tears when I think about a lifetime of loving experiences with my wife. I have never ever met anyone else quite like her and I'm extremely sad that she is gone, and I have to live for the remainder of my life without her. I cry without shame when I think of her, and it may be a very long time before I can think about her, talk about her or even see her name without getting emotional.

Others can be stoic, internalizing their grief without tears. Grieving is an unpredictable process that is unique to everyone, and it is difficult to know how to react to other people when they are in the grieving process.

For instance, quite a few people have said to me, "you will get through this period because you are so strong." They have no idea how lost I feel and how disinterested I have become in almost everything that used to excite me. No matter what I try to do, memories of Peggy interrupt my thought process and destroy whatever pleasure I might have gotten out of whatever it was I was doing at that moment. For sure, I don't put on a happy face to camouflage how I feel at any given second. What you see is what you get, tears and all, and I am not embarrassed by it. What's more, I don't expect that to change any time soon.

I don't know what is in store for me as I try to move through this cloud of unhappiness. I don't yet know whether I will go through all five stages, skip some or add more. What may be most important is that we recognize that all forms of grieving are part of a normal, natural, and necessary process, as we react to the loss of a loved one. Each of us is unique and our relationship with our loved ones is also unique.

Dr. David B. Feldman, an author, speaker, and professor of counseling psychology at Santa Clara University, in California, in "Why Five Stages of Grief are Wrong" in **Psychology Today**, says that grief is not that simple. He states that no one should be self-critical because he or she does not go through all five stages or doesn't grieve in that order.

Feldman maintains that no matter what our unique grieving process may be, there are three important things to keep in mind. The first he claims is that in moderate amounts, denial can be healthy, but fully facing the reality that a loved one has died is ultimately good for us. Denial becomes unhealthy only when it is ongoing and becomes unshakeable.

The second thing to keep in mind is that grief can shake our faith in the world. We are particularly stressed when we see bad things happen to good people. That isn't supposed to happen in an orderly world. The loss of someone you love can challenge your beliefs in fairness and equality. But Feldman points out that death is neither fair nor unfair. It's simply a reality we must all face eventually.

Feldman's third lesson is that grief usually leads to acceptance, which is Kuber-Ross's final stage. He writes: "Although most people never stop missing their departed loved ones, the painful emotions they feel shortly after the death almost certainly eventually soften." Almost everyone I've discussed this with who has suffered the loss of a loved one, confirmed for me that the pain never leaves, but lessens over time.

Having discussed this with a number of these people, it seems to me that nobody has any real idea how long grief should take. Each of them said he or she will never stop grieving, but they each said the worst part took a lot longer than they thought it would, something between one and two years. Several are still grieving after three or four years.

It is almost impossible for anyone to predict specifically what is normal for each of us. Some people go through all the predicted stages of grieving and some only go through some of these stages. What is evident to me is that no one should feel guilty for not going through all five stages sequentially, or skipping some stages altogether.

The grieving stages are a guideline and are not set in stone. It is important that the person who has lost a loved one knows that however he or she feels is okay. He or she does not have to go through a predictable form of grief. Grieving is a very personal experience and I'm only writing about it from my perspective based on how my wife and I reacted to her illness and my own experiences when she died.

I don't seem to be going through all five stages, or perhaps I just imagine I'm not going through them. Perhaps what I define as disappointment is really anger, even though I don't really feel angry. I also find that at any given moment I might be experiencing several stages of grief simultaneously. For instance, at times I experienced denial and disappointment (anger) at the same time. My guess is that none of the traditional stages of grief are necessarily isolated from each other, and how we react to them may be determined by our own unique personality or character makeup.

Again, perhaps the most important thing to remember during the first stage is this: grieving is a personal process that has no time limit, or one "right way" to do it. It isn't always understandable in the moment. I frequently don't understand the flood of emotions I have, although they sometimes become clearer after I've experienced them. Keep in mind that everything is normal and nothing is normal. All of our grief experiences are unique.

Feldman's final comment is perhaps the most relevant. "Grief isn't a race to the finish line, and it isn't a contest to see who fits Kubler-Ross's stages best. It's a natural, though emotionally difficult, part of life, and one that can't be easily explained by five simple stages." So read these stages understanding that they may not be complete or relevant in every stage to whatever it is you are going through as you read this book.

Also, there are a lot of myths about grieving, and some of your very best friends might try to convince you that they are real and must be addressed. Keep in mind these myths about grief that Kenneth C. Haugk lists in his booklet, **A Time To Grieve**.

Myth: People with a strong faith don't grieve.

Myth: A strong person should be able to get through a loss without showing emotion.

Myth: You should be pretty much back to normal after two or three months.

Myth: If you express intense feelings, you're losing control of yourself.

Myth: Crying is a sign of weakness.

Myth: Grief gets easier as you grow older.

Myth: Getting angry at God means you have a weak faith.

Myth: You can tell how much a person loved the one who died by how deeply and long the person grieves the loss.

Myth: Losing an infant doesn't hurt because parents didn't have time to get to know the child.

Myth: Resolving your grief means putting your loved one out of your mind and moving on with your life.

Myth: A strong person should be able to deal with grief alone.

Myth: Christians shouldn't grieve if they know their loved one is in heaven. They should only feel joy.

Myth: It's better to deal with grief intellectually than emotionally.

Myth: Only immediate family members will experience significant grief.

Myth: Continuing to talk about the person who died only makes the pain last longer.

Myth: Grief proceeds through very predictable and orderly stages.

Myth: After a loved one has died, you can never be happy again.

These myths are believed by a lot of people, some of who may spring them on you as fact. Try to not be intimidated by people who seem to be genuinely concerned about you, but simply don't really know what they are talking about. They mean well, but you have to take their comments "with a grain of salt." That means you can accept their well-intentioned comments, while maintaining a degree of skepticism about the truth.

You may find that a lot of your friends, who have not studied dying or grief, believe a lot of these myths, so just listen to them, knowing they are trying to be helpful, but understand that few if any of them can truly appreciate what you are going thorough or how best to deal with your pain.

I know from my own experience that well-meaning people sometimes say unimaginably hurtful, insensitive things unintentionally. They just do not understand what the person who is grieving is going through, and do not realize that thoughtless comments just add to the pain of grieving. And, while it may be difficult, the grieving person must try to not take offense from such comments, particularly when they come from very close personal friends who don't even know they are adding to the pain.

CHAPTER THREE

Stage One—Denial and Isolation

According to Julie Axelrod, the stages of grief are universal and are experienced by people from all walks of life. Denial is the very first stage that happens right after a loved one dies. Your initial thought may be that "this just can't be happening," or "why, Lord, is this some form of punishment for something I've done or forgot to do?" You might even begin to think you are going crazy because you can't find any rational reason for the predicament in which you and your spouse find yourselves.

But, denial is really none of these. Denial is a brief way of dealing with an overwhelming sense of sadness and loss that can't be rationalized in any acceptable way. I don't know anyone who believes the Lord takes people to heaven as a punishment for people on earth. That is simply an irrational way to approach the death of a loved one, or the love of our Lord. God is not going to kill your spouse because He is mad at you!

After loving each other for 62 years, the thought of being permanently separated from the love of my life is stifling. I can't even imagine how I am going to live in this world without my love. It is the most unimaginable thing I have ever had to deal with.

Initially I sometimes had trouble breathing, and I sometimes still find myself crying at even the sight of her name on a piece of paper or on envelopes that came in the mail. I find myself asking the Lord why he took her at this stage of our life. Why couldn't he let her live a bit longer, or better yet, why didn't he find a way to take us home together? I hate anything that focuses me exclusively on Peggy and starts tears that leave me feeling scared and alone.

Except for not abandoning our home, for a while I quit going to a lot of the places we frequented before her illness, e.g., church, restaurants and other places in which we loved to relax. Her aura lingered almost everywhere we had ever enjoyed each other's company. I still have trouble walking past my memories of her in our home. However, I sometimes walk into her closet and stand there for a few minutes, because I can still smell her presence there. I can't stay in there too long though, because it starts a flood of tears that I cannot control.

These things force me to acknowledge the reality of her death, which almost instantly brings tears running down my cheeks. The emotional pain these memories produce are something I never even considered during the 18-months she struggled with cancer. They came as a shock after she died, and I wasn't prepared for them. In truth, I still have trouble accepting the reality that I will never see her again in this lifetime.

Somehow, I always thought the cancer would go into remission and she would survive. After all, she had gone through more than a year of very strong chemotherapy. I thought surely the strong medications would prolong her life and give us a few more years. Boy, was I wrong. The strong medications didn't even slow down the cancerous curse as it continued its battle to kill my wife.

I was with her the moment she died, and could not deny her death, but I can sure agree with the feelings of isolation that immediately overwhelmed me. Fortunately, a friend and his wife were in the room at that time too. They immediately approached me and said, "Don, don't go home tonight. Come stay with us for awhile."

I accepted their offer and stayed with them for five days. It took that long for me to feel ready to face my home with all the immediate memories lurking in every room.

When I felt ready to go home, I was overcome with feelings of loneliness. While thinking of a lost loved one, it is possible to feel lonely even while sitting with a crowd of people. The mind can block out all the caring people around you while you focus selectively on the person you lost and the misery being felt in that moment. Some people have a difficult time understanding how that can be. But, trust me, it happened to me frequently over the first few months after her death.

One day Peggy was alive, and maintained her sense of humor, and the next day she was gone. I was shocked, even though I had watched her struggle with metastatic ovarian cancer for nearly 18 months. I doubt there is any way to prepare for that inevitable time when you must acknowledge the reality of death, while dealing with the emotional turmoil that reality causes. I simply was not ready to accept my wife's death.

Even though I had frequently sat all day watching chemotherapy being infused into her body, I didn't really think that death was lurking so closely to our lives. I doubt I would have been ready even if a doctor had predicted it a year in advance. Death came as a shock to me even though we knew it was coming. We just didn't have a specific date, and for sure I wasn't ready for it when it came.

When she died, while I didn't deny her death, it was difficult for me to accept the reality of it emotionally. Intellectually there was no way to deny what I had personally witnessed. One minute I could hear her breathing and the next minute she was deathly quiet.

The hospice nurse came into the room and checked her with a stethoscope and immediately told me she had passed. She had been motionless most of the day and the only evidence I had that she was still alive was her breathing. At the risk of sounding redundant, I was shocked at how quickly I lost her. I suspect there simply is no way to adequately prepare for the death of a loved one.

After spending five days with fiends, I returned home, and was overwhelmed because I could see her in every room. There was evidence of her existence everywhere I looked. Pictures, clothes, and favorite things are everywhere as immediate reminders of our 62-year love affair.

When I drove around town, I could feel her presence in restaurants we frequented and stores we favored. She was suddenly everywhere, in ways that were extremely difficult for me to deal with. I could tell that some of my friends were concerned with my grief, but they were all very kind.

I felt tremendously depressed and had a hard time accepting that I would never see her again in this lifetime. I would start crying at even a passing thought of her. What got to me the most was acknowledging that to see her again I must first die so we can be reunited in heaven. That may be a belief unique to Christians, but it brings both sadness and comfort to me. Sadness because the wait could be quite long, yet comfort because I know the Bible says we eventually will be reunited in heaven.

The trouble I have with it is the fact that I have my mother's genes and she lived to age 92. I am now 83. If I live that long, and it is conceivable that I could live even longer than that, it would mean that I will likely spend another eight or ten years alone, without Peggy, before I can be reunited with her in heaven.

That is a possibility I acknowledge, but one I have a difficult time processing even today because of my own health history. In 1989 I had a massive heart attack and almost died three times. It left me with only half a heart, literally. The heart attack killed the bottom half of my heart. It left me with the knowledge that I could only put so much stress on my heart without feeling chest pains. Indeed, I had a pacemaker for six years and then had it replaced with another one for six years, and finally had the pacemaker replaced by an implanted defibrillator that also functions as a pacemaker. In theory, if my heart should stop the defibrillator will kick start it again!

I have survived 30 years with half a heart, mainly because I have a good cardiologist, good medicines and I'm careful about how much stress I place on the damaged heart. I have to pace myself. I do everything slowly. I walk slowly and I manage my life slowly. If I even make my bed too fast I get severe chest pains that require me to stop for a period. I am amazed that I have lasted so long.

In fact Peggy and I both thought that because of my heart and the fact that I am also an insulin-dependent diabetic with peripheral diabetic neuropathy in both feet, I would be the first to die. Initially, I didn't think I would ever live to see age 65, but here I am at age 83. Many years ago the Veterans Administration confirmed for me that all of my health issues stem from my exposure to Agent Orange in South Vietnam.

Throughout 1974, I served with the Joint Casualty Resolution Center, which was a joint–service operation responsible for finding Americans who were missing-in-action. Our unit was made up of about 80 percent Army Special Forces personnel, another 15 percent Army mortuary affairs personnel, and five percent people like me from other services. I accompanied casualty resolution teams all over South Vietnam where we located American servicemen who had died in combat, but whose bodies had never been recovered.

Once we located them we had to exhume their remains and take the remains to our Central Identification Laboratory, where they could be identified and their next of kin could be notified.

The Special Forces personnel protected us, the mortuary affairs personnel did the exhumation and, as an Air Force public affairs officer, I handled the international press who always seemed to find us and always had lots of questions. I was the interface with the press, both for the United States generally and for the U.S Embassies in South Vietnam and Thailand, before and after the exhumations occurred. It was one of my favored military assignments, because we helped bring closure to grieving families.

Since our casualty resolution efforts took us all over South Vietnam, we necessarily travelled thorough areas that had previously been sprayed with Agent Orange, which is how I became exposed. Agent Orange was an exceptionally good defoliant; unfortunately we didn't have any idea how dangerous it would be to our own personnel who might later walk through areas that had been sprayed with it.

However, back to Peggy, just three months before her cancer took a turn for the worse, she begged me to lose my belly. She was scared to death I would die before she would. As it turns out I just keep chugging along with half a heart, even though my belly does really need to be reduced.

The trouble I have with outliving Peggy by eight or ten years is the enormous emotional pain that could last as long as 3,650 days. That's how many days are in ten years. I have a friend whose wife died eight years ago. When I asked him how long the grieving process lasted for him, he paused to think for a minute and then said: "I will never stop grieving, but the most difficult time was the first two years. " Others I've asked have said a whole slew of different time periods. There just is no set time period for grieving.

In God's time eight or ten years are insignificant periods when contrasted with eternity, yet for me time goes slowly without Peggy by my side. Even so, I can rationalize that time only looks far off when one tries to peer into the future. Looking back the perspective of time is much different.

When senior citizens recall how anxious they were to reach age 16 or age 21, they might wonder why they felt so much anxiety waiting, because when looking back, time is usually gone in a flash. I can intellectually explain that right now, without accepting it emotionally. Because I would like to join my wife today, even the thought of eight or ten more years into the future is unbearable.

I remember how boldly we faced the future when we married in 1959, believing we had an eternity in front of us to love each other. We were poor, but we were thrilled at the prospect of spending a lifetime together. Over the years I became fairly successful, retiring as the corporate director of Public Affairs for the General Dynamics Corporation, which gave me two retirements, one from the military and one from General Dynamics. Of course, I also have Social Security benefits.

But, while Peggy was going through chemotherapy, none of that mattered. All I could think about was how fast our life together had passed. Looking back I kept thinking, "Where did all those years go? How did we arrive at the gates of heaven so quickly? How will I survive my remaining time on earth without the most important person in my life?"

Christians will have no trouble with those rationalizations. Even though Roman Catholics and Protestants differ dramatically in the rituals they perform, they share the same salvation message, with Heaven as the ultimate goal. It is an article of faith that all Christians believe at the moment of death God will judge us, and we will be selected by Him to spend all of eternity in either Heaven or Hell. A discussion of the criteria for selection to either destination would be better discussed in a separate writing, as would the concept of death as taught by other religions.

I can't imagine any two people deeply in love not being disappointed with God when He takes one of them home, while leaving the other one behind. I kept thinking, why didn't God find a way to take us home together? Only He knows how much we love each other. What's the point of separating us at the end, and why would He want me to live alone, without her, for the rest of my life?

But, even with all of my analyzing and rationalizing I have never denied the reality of what was happening. I simply hoped and prayed that He would give us an extension on our life together. We were not so fortunate.

After months of trying to adjust to living life alone, I can understand why some people get angry with God. But for me, anger was simply not a recognizable part of my grief.

However, shock and disappointment were a definite part of my grieving process. Even knowing my Peggy was going to die, it was a huge shock when it actually happened, and I can understand how that shock for many people can manifest itself in a form of extreme anger.

I suppose there is really not a lot of difference between anger and disappointment. Certainly anyone who is deeply disappointed could find that anger is a natural accompaniment. But for some reason I have not yet rationalized, I can't get mad at a God who gave me so many wonderful years with my sweet wife.

Anger for many people might be easy to understand, but for me anger simply wasn't a part of my grieving process. Even now, after three months without my Peggy, I still can't get angry with God. All I can do is beg Him to not wait very long to take me up there to be with her.

One thing I did learn in the process of Peggy dying is that it would not be helpful to try to grieve the way someone else grieved. Comparisons don't help because grieving is so personal. Nobody else can truly imagine how Peggy's death is affecting me, and I can't pattern my grief based on how somebody else grieved.

The truth is I probably will not know the full effect of grief for many more months, or perhaps even years. My love was and is so singularly focused on Peggy that I cannot even conceive of me ever loving another woman the way I love Peggy. My singular focus is going to be waiting for God to reunite us in Heaven.

To a psychologist that may be something to analyze negatively, but for me it is a natural progression of our mutual love. Just as I could not even imagine loving another person the way I loved her, I can't imagine another Peggy in my life during the time I have left on Earth. It is simply going to be a period of waiting, however long, to be with her again. Some days waiting is painful and sad, but others are filled with the support of friends who will make the wait more tolerable.

CHAPTER FOUR

Stage Two—Anger

Anger is thought to be a necessary stage of the healing process; but; as mentioned earlier, not all people go through all five stages. Anger is a common form of anxiety for many people when they lose a loved one. It is understandable how people can be mad at God for taking away someone they desperately love.

It is common for Christian friends to plead with me to pray to God for healing, at this difficult time. However, for me that initially seemed a bit like an oxymoron, asking God to heal the pain He caused when He took away the most important person in my life. But, in truth, I can understand why He might want to take a loved one to Heaven.

In Peggy's case, as I mentioned in the second chapter, she devoted two or three hours every single day to studying God's words in the Bible. Jesus Christ was the central focus of her life, and as death approached, she simply welcomed it, all the while knowing full well that her death would deal a crushing blow to me. She acknowledged that she knew how much I would suffer, and that she hated the thought of leaving me, but she was very tired and ready for heaven, with no fear or trepidation.

Her relationship with Jesus Christ came before everything and everyone else in her life, including me, other members of our family, and all other considerations, no matter how important they may seem to be at any moment. Jesus Christ was very real to Peggy, and she prayed every day that He would eventually take her to Heaven. She never once showed any apprehension or anxiety as she approached death. She faced it as calmly as I've ever seen anyone face it, and I saw plenty of men face death in South Vietnam. She was absolutely ready to die and meet Jesus Christ.

While I'm sure she included me in her daily prayers, she never pushed me to join her in her daily bible study. She knew I was not as bible conscious as she was, even though I am a weekly volunteer in our church.

I have been ushering in our church, going to bible study classes, and otherwise participating in the weekly Christian programs available for followers of Jesus Christ ever since I started attending Calvary Chapel Viera in 2004. Even now, I am attending a 15-week course titled Grief Share at my church.

But, I am quick to acknowledge that nothing I ever did in life came even close to the daily personal relationship Peggy felt she had with Jesus Christ. And I can muster no anger for God because he gave me so many exciting and breathtaking years with this sweet, wonderful woman. There is simply no way I could ever be angry with a God who cared enough to provide me with this exceptional wife to share my life with for so many years.

While it's true I often feel isolated and alone since Peggy died, and am getting back to my daily life, it has not been easy. I am thrilled that Peggy is in Heaven, even as I suffer great emotional pain over her absence. It is somewhat comforting to know that I will eventually be reunited with her. What is disconcerting is not knowing how long that wait might take.

We had a beautiful one-hour memorial service for Peggy, with exceptional music she had picked out for the service. I spoke first for about 15 minutes, covering our absolutely wonderful life and how much I am going to miss this exceptional woman.

Four friends who remembered special moments of their lifetime experiences with her followed me. Each of the four speakers related different aspects of her personality, yet they were all accurate reflections of her character. She was a complex, yet beautiful woman who made friends easily. The friends who spoke made it clear to the audience that Peggy was an exceptionally lovable Christ follower.

At her memorial nearly 300 people attended to say goodbye. Many of them said to me that it was the most beautiful funeral service they had ever attended. Pastor Kevin Winn was magnificent in his memorializing of Peggy. He knew and loved Peggy, just as she and I shared a Christian love for him. I can't imagine a funeral or memorial service going any better than the one we held for Peggy.

People who attended the memorial service were impressed with how Pastor Winn conducted it. In fact, I had many of them say to me after the service that they want Pastor Winn to handle their family funerals. All in all, I'm sure Peggy was happy as she watched from Heaven, if such a thing is possible.

Actually, she made all the arrangements long before she died. Because she didn't want me to have to handle the details, she met with our church pastor and personally selected Pastor Winn to officiate and met with the music director to select the music she wanted at her service. All I had to do at the memorial was to set up the urn, a photo of us together, and place her Bible on display along with a collage of our life together that she had also commissioned. And, of course I had to write the eulogy of my remembrance of she and I together. It was a love story that I proudly explained to those who attended the memorial.

I can understand, however, how someone else might be extremely angry with God for taking away the very essence of his or her life. Anger can be a defensive reaction to something or someone who is thought to be a cause of the pain that provoked the anger, and that anger is no less real when the person who caused it is Jesus Christ.

Instead of anger, I felt lost, without a sense of direction or purpose in life. The reality of my loss didn't completely hit me for a while. But, eventually it hit me extremely hard. In addition to crying more than I like to admit, I often had dreams of happy times with Peggy, and

I found myself staying in bed much longer than usual. Sleep was an escape. While I normally sleep seven or eight hours each night, I found myself sleeping 10 or 11 hours each night for quite a while.

I often heard usual sounds in the house and found myself thinking they were sounds of Peggy doing something. A few times I caught myself yelling, "is that you honey?" Of course, I knew immediately the sounds were normal house sounds and were not related to Peggy. Then I felt embarrassed for projecting Peggy on to the sounds. It was a form of desperation, hoping against hope that Peggy was still with me. Only someone who has gone through a similar experience can imagine how painful it is.

I should have realized I was going through a terrible amount of stress. I had a headache and upset stomach for over a month, and I sometimes found it difficult to concentrate. Peggy kept interrupting my thoughts and I sometimes found it difficult to regain my focus by moving away from those thoughts.

Sometimes I would get angry with myself for being such a fool, knowing full well that Peggy is in Heaven. Then I would ease up on myself, knowing that what I was going through was quite normal. Even though in the Bible God brought back to life at least eight different people, there is no evidence of Him doing anything like that in recent history. Wishing for a God inspired miracle goes against the grain when what Peggy went through was quite normal for cancer patients, and getting angry at God or her doctors or anyone else would be futile and meaningless.

The simple truth is this: except for suicides, God decides all births and deaths, and it does no good to be angry with Him. Death is inevitable for all of us. What is questionable and for which there is no answer is this: why do some people die suddenly from a heart attack or stroke or some other malady, while others take months or even years to die? Why do some people die quickly, without any suffering, while others die slowly, with months and months of pain and suffering?

In my wife's case, she suffered throughout her 18-month ordeal, but claimed she never had any pain. I never quite understood that because for over a year she was miserable for the first week after she took chemotherapy. She couldn't even get out of bed during that week. Yet, she claimed she was miserable but had no pain throughout her ordeal.

I can believe that for her last month on earth. She was so weak she couldn't even get out of her chair. For her to go to the bathroom, I had to lift her out of her chair and take her there, and when she was finished I had to repeat the process. But she never once complained of any pain or inconvenience, only how uncomfortable it was.

As I mentioned earlier, the Hospice Center gave her morphine and a sedative as soon as she arrived at its center, and she died within 28-hours after her arrival. I can only imagine the pain I would still be suffering if she had died at home and I had to face that room every day. As it is, it is difficult for me to face her study because there is so much of her in it. I still have not cleared out her room and don't know when I might do it.

But it was hard to believe she felt no pain right to the end, when she was miserable and couldn't get out of bed every three weeks during her 18-month struggle. Nevertheless, I took her word for that fact and the fact that she never ever displayed any form of anger throughout those months. I would watch her suffer and think, "Why isn't she angry with God?"

From time to time I had enough disappointment, anger, or both for the two of us. I couldn't then and can't now understand why our God would let such a wonderful Christ-follower suffer for 18 months before taking her home to be with Him. It's like the big question Christians often ask, why does God allow bad things to happen to good people. Of course there will never be a good answer to that question.

One of my concerns is that my mother died at age 92, within 30 minutes after her heart attack, while my sweet, wonderful wife suffered for months. There is simply no way I can rationalize that difference. That doesn't mean I think my mother should have suffered longer, it's just that there seems to be a huge imbalance in the way God treats us.

In truth, even though we saw Peggy's death coming for quite some time, the reality of it was just as much of a shock for me as my mother's death, which was truly unexpected. I don't think there is any way I could have prepared for Peggy's death no matter how much notice I might have had.

I lost the most important person in the world to me, and there just is no way to prepare for that no matter how long the illness or what the doctors tell you. I am only disappointed that He has left me here to struggle with her memories for God only knows how long, when I want desperately to be with her.

However, I have to wait for God to do his magic, because there is simply no way I could commit suicide and risk a permanent separation from Peggy. Everything must happen in God's time!

CHAPTER FIVE

Stage Three—Bargaining

There are lots of ways people bargain with God at such times as these. You do that for me God and I'll do this for you. Over the period that Peggy suffered with ovarian cancer, I must have tried to bargain with God at least a dozen or more times, although I can't remember a time when I thought she was bargaining with Him. She just was not interested in bargaining with God, because she knew in her heart that she was merely days away from meeting him personally.

On the other hand, I would do anything he asked of me if he would only spare her life and give us more time together. While I knew the reality of her approaching death, I just could not believe it was going to happen. I pleaded and begged with God to give us more time, or to take me with her. But, it eventually became clear to me that no matter how much I begged Him, He was not going to grant me that wish.

It seemed very simple to me. With all of God's power it would be a very modest thing for Him to give us a few more years together. What I was asking was not something difficult for Him. I just wanted Him to restore our life together; to give us a couple of more years together; maybe even find a way to take us home together.

It seemed to me there was a close relationship between my disappointment (anger) with God and my efforts to bargain with Him.

What I finally came to realize is that I had nothing to bargain with, nothing He wanted at the moment.

I could see how taking Peggy home to be with Him was far more important than anything I could promise Him. Certainly she could be more important to Him than leaving her to be with me. It began to seem idiotic to say to God, "If you let me keep Peggy for a few more years I'll (fill in the words)." Everything I thought I might promise God seemed trivial and unimportant. Besides, I don't know what made me think God would be susceptible to bargaining.

I didn't know what else to do to make the pain go away. Life without my Peggy was and still is emotionally overwhelming. Sometimes, even now, I'm not sure how I'm going to get through the day. I never dreamed that dealing with the grief would be so difficult and take so long. I am now finding out that for many people it takes years. When I consider that she has been gone more than three months and it still seems like she died yesterday, it becomes fairly clear to me that grief is not something I'm going to get over quickly.

I'm sure I'm not the first person to think perhaps God isn't listening to me or perhaps He just doesn't care about me. He has seven and a half billion people to worry about, and I'm pretty insignificant. I have prayed as fervently as I know how, I have shouted and yelled at God, I have pleaded with Him and begged Him, I have promised Him everything I can think of that is of any consequence, but it often appears as though he either doesn't hear me or just doesn't care about my concerns.

As I watched Peggy slide into the final stages of her life, I wondered, without asking her, why she didn't seem to be the least bit upset that death was approaching rapidly and there was nothing either of us could do about it.

As it turned out, she was praying for heaven, not for remission. She was very, very tired and uncomfortable, and saw no other way out of her dilemma, except death. Besides, she was a dedicated Christ follower and was absolutely sure of where she was going. She was definitely a whole lot stronger at that point than I was. I was approaching "basket case" and continued to beg.

Of course, mine was an egotistical approach to prayer. I know He hears me and of course He cares, but sometimes what I want or the timing of what I want just isn't on His schedule. Sometimes we forget that God does everything on His own time.

I haven't figured out yet what it meant that He took Peggy home at this particular time. I have no idea what He wants me to do without her. I can't believe He just wants me to be unhappy. That is a perverse thought that is more of a reflection on me than on Him. But, I can honestly say I have never been more unhappy than I am now, without her and knowing I have nothing to bargain with.

The bottom line is really quite simple. Either He will grant my prayer wish or He won't. If He doesn't, I have no alternative other than to live out the life He gave me for as long as His time-line dictates.

According to David A. DePra in his article *"Bargaining With God,"* in **The Good News-Home**, the truth is, God wants to ultimately set us free from all bargaining with Him. And if we allow Him to do so, then He will be free to give us Himself, and everything else that is a part of His will. In short, if we let go and trust God, we end up with everything we might have otherwise tried to bargain for.

Sometimes we try to bargain with God without specifically thinking of it as bargaining. In "More Than We Bargained For," in a series by Vic Folkert on March 22, 2018, he illustrates this idea with the following examples:

> …if we work hard and live ethically, will God bless us with success?
>
> …if we invest time in our children, live godly lives, and do the best we can, will we have good kids?
>
> …if we eat vegetables, watch our weight, work out and take care of our bodies, will we be healthy?

The truth is that God doesn't do bargains. That whole idea is ridiculous. Why should God bargain? What could we possibly offer Him that He doesn't already have? There is no *quid pro quo* in our relationship with God.

The closest thing I can think of that might seem to be a bargain is when we follow the rules He has given us to live by, and the example of his son, Jesus Christ, then ask for His help to live by his rules, and expect to spend eternity in heaven as a result of our obedience to His word. Even that would not be a bargain. Nothing we ever do will qualify us for Heaven. There is no way we can merit Heaven. Only God's grace makes that possible.

Nevertheless, bargaining seems to be ingrained in us. I doubt there is anyone who has not tried to bargain with God. It's almost as natural as breathing. I suspect most, if not all of us, when faced with desperate or difficult situations, have tried to persuade God to rescue us by offering to do something we think would please Him.

I doubt I have ever had any bargaining chips in my entire life. We all fool ourselves from time to time thinking we can bargain with God. In reality, it is the epitome of arrogance to think that we can bargain with Him. Nevertheless, I know that I would have done anything God asked of me to spare my wife's life. I also know there is nothing I could do that would equal the value of her life either to Him or to me.

When we try to bargain with God we mostly fail to understand that we have absolutely no leverage. He created us and has ultimate authority over our lives. That means He can have whatever he wants from us, whenever He wants it, without bargaining.

Bargaining generally occurs between two people having similar strengths and weaknesses. There is no scenario in which that could occur between God and us. We simply fool ourselves when we think we are bargaining with Him.

The **Psychology Dictionary** defines bargaining as an attempt between two parties to agree on terms and to resolve conflict. In the process, limited resources are traded in exchange for a particular benefit - to negotiate terms and arrive at a mutual agreement. It is not considered bargaining if one side holds all the advantages. Which means, almost by definition, despite what many people think, there is no way we can bargain with God.

Allan R. Bevere, Pastor of the first United Methodist Church in Ashland, Ohio, and a Professional Fellow in Theology at Ashland Theological Seminary, also in Ashland, and the author of **The Politics of Witness**, says "Let me suggest that it is never okay to bargain with God, because in bargaining with God we think we get to set the parameters of the deal, not the Almighty."

> "When one looks in the bible at the covenants God makes with his people, it is God who sets the terms of the covenants and they are non—negotiable. God says, 'this is what I will do for you; here is what you will do.' There is no bargaining here. What God has promised is not in doubt and what we are to do is not in doubt; whether or not we do it is another matter, but there is no bargaining—only God's promises and stipulations, and our obedience."

In my opinion it is self-delusional to believe it is possible to bargain with God. In the end, God does what God wants. He is probably overjoyed when we do what He wants, but in the end what matters is what God wants, not what we want. The best approach is to always do what we are sure God wants us to do, and not try to bargain with Him.

CHAPTER SIX

Stage Four—Depression

Steve Bressert, Ph.D, in a **Psych Central** article, "Depression Symptoms" (Major Depressive Disorder), describes depression like this:

> The symptoms of depression—technically referred to as major depressive disorder—are characterized by an overwhelming feeling of sadness, isolation, and despair that lasts two weeks or longer at a time. Depression isn't just an occasional feeling of being sad or lonely, like most people experience from time to time. Instead, a person who has depression feels like they've sunk into a deep, dark hole with no way out—and no hope for things ever changing.

Bressert characterizes clinical depression by the presence of five or more of these depressive symptoms:

- Depressed mood most of the day, nearly every day.
- Markedly diminished interest or pleasure in almost any activity.
- Significant weight loss when not dieting or weight gain.
- Insomnia. The inability to sleep or to stay asleep.

- Problem sitting still, restlessness, pacing, or picking at one's clothes.
- Fatigue, tiredness, or loss of energy nearly every day.
- Feelings of worthlessness or excessive or inappropriate guilt nearly every day.
- Diminished ability to think or concentrate, or indecisiveness, nearly every day.
- Recurrent thoughts of death, recurrent suicidal ideas without a specific plan, or suicide attempt or specific plan to do so.

I found that any of these symptoms could occur with me over a period of time in no particular order. Certainly a major depression can occur when a person suffers from a major episode of bereavement or grief for the loss of a loved one.

However, I found as it relates to me, that there is a considerable difference between general depression, which we all experience from time to time, and the horrific depression **Psych Central** describes. Certainly my depression was something in between the two kinds. It took about a week for the reality of my wife's death to finally settle in and overwhelm me with sadness and feelings of loneliness and isolation.

I knew she was gone and would never return, but for a few days I was distracted by the wonderful care I received from friends. Their concerns diverted my attention from the immediacy of an emotional reaction to Peggy's death. However, once I returned home and faced the reminders of Peggy's presence in each room and the certain knowledge that she would never return to give me a hug and kiss, fix a shade, prepare a meal, watch TV with me, wash clothes, go to church, or any one of a dozen different personal reminders of her passing, I broke down and cried, and I continue to cry at various times daily. The periods between crying are getting longer, but it is still a daily ritual that I don't seem to have any control over.

Remember that I learned from several of Peggy's friends that she had told them to watch after me when she died because she knew I would become a "basket case." She knew me well. I hope she can look down from Heaven and watch my reaction and recovery. Part of the evidence of my being a basket case was certainly copious amounts of water flowing down my cheeks every day.

I don't mean a couple of tears; I mean a deluge of water that would not stop. I simply could not get my mind off of the fact that I would never again in this world see the wonderful woman who was the love of my life, my constant companion, my better half, and the lovely woman whom God provided to share my life with forever.

While my reaction to her death is improving from week to week, I still find, after more than three months, I have little or no control over my tears. Even as I write this chapter, I can barely see the screen through the water flooding my eyes, and I have no idea how long it will take to get through an entire day without crying.

There are times I envy the stoic folks who shed no tears, but that is not who I am. I am and have always been emotional and have never subscribed to the philosophy that says, "boys and men don't cry." Love has no bounds, and I am not embarrassed to cry over losing Peggy. There will never ever be anyone in my life to compare with the love I have always felt for her.

My friends at church wondered what happened to me because I stopped going to church for about four months. Because Peggy had no functional immune system, I could not risk "catching something" at church while ushering and bringing it home to her. Even a cold could have killed her. So, I stopped going to church for about two months before she died.

After she died, I was so overcome with grief that I couldn't think about her without crying. So I stayed home for another two months until I felt like I could hug people and answer obvious questions about how I'm doing, or to explain what happened to Peggy, when people who didn't know she had died, asked how she was doing.

Even after four months away from church, I wasn't sure how I would hold up when neighbors and people at church asked about Peggy. As it turned out, about two months after her death a lot of the depression lifted, and I felt like I could return to ushering at church. I was mostly right until I had to explain to many church friends why they hadn't seen Peggy or me for so long. Then I would have a difficult time talking, and I could feel myself weeping a bit, but everyone understood and was wonderfully supportive.

One of the things we need to keep in mind as we discuss depression is that grief can trigger depression, but not everyone who grieves will experience depression. There are notable differences between grieving and depression.

According to an article in **Health Line** Newsletter, "Coping With Depression After a Loved One's Death," dated June 27, 2017, written by Rachel Nall, RN, BSN, CCRN, and medically reviewed by Timothy J. Legg, PhD, CRNP, there are several major and important differences between grief and depression.

Depressed people tend to feel depressed all the time, while people who grieve can have symptoms that mimic depression, but those symptoms can fluctuate or come in waves. Grief is not necessarily a full-time, constant problem that needs medical attention. Severe depression can require specific medical attention over a period of time.

People who are grieving can accept help from family and friends, while depressed people may isolate themselves and shun others. People who are grieving may still be able to go to work or school or participate in social activities, however, clinically depressed people may experience symptoms so severe that they are unable to go to work or do important tasks and may need specific medical help to recover.

With grief, depression, or both, it is important to remember that there can be a very good long-term outlook. As Ms. Nall relates, "Losing a loved one doesn't mean your life is over, but it does mean things will be very different. Seeking help and support can help you feel better. With time, you can find healing that will help you move forward with your life, while also celebrating your loved one's memory"

However, if you find that nothing seems to help you move forward with your life and you seem to be stuck in a permanent form of extreme depression, it is important to seek medical help from a professional. That is usually not necessary for someone who is just grieving, but is not clinically depressed; but it is almost always necessary for people who are clinically depressed.

CHAPTER SEVEN

Stage Five—Acceptance

The last stage of grief identified by Kubler-Ross is acceptance. It is not acceptance in the sense that it's okay that your husband or wife died, but in the sense that, given enough time to recover, you are going to be okay. You may still grieve from time to time, as images, people, or events remind you of the death of your loved one, but in the main you can establish a new normal.

In a **PSYCOM** article, "The Five Stages of Grief, An Examination of the Kubler-Ross Model," by Christina Gregory, PhD, she points out that "in this stage, your emotions may begin to stabilize. You come to terms with the fact that the 'new' reality is that your partner is never coming back...and that you're okay with that. It's not a good thing, but it's something you can live with."

During this period I have good days and bad days and good days again. In fact, I am already experiencing this phenomenon on an ongoing basis. It doesn't mean that after a series of good days, I will never have a bad day again. I've already had that happen to me too. After a period when I thought I was on the road to recovery, I suddenly had a day where I saw something that reminded me of an especially happy time with Peggy and suddenly I was uncontrollably sad and the tears returned. I've even had that happen as I walk through our house and glimpse at a photo of us doing something that we really enjoyed doing earlier in our marriage.

I am sure this is going to happen many more times during the course of the next year or two. I have no illusions about how quickly I will be able to adjust to the absence of Peggy in my life, because she was my main focus for 62 years, and I love her ever more even today. It isn't the kind of love that can be broken even temporarily; it is constant and never changing.

But, in this stage, I am re-engaging with friends in my neighborhood and at church and hoping to establish a new reality for me. I go to breakfast almost weekly with two dear friends. Does that mean I will never have those suddenly sad days any more? Of course not! It means I am adjusting to the reality that while Peggy cannot be replaced, I must move on with my life, while waiting for the day when I will be reunited with her in Heaven.

I view that as a positive, not a negative thought. I doubt the day will ever come when I can think of our reunion without hoping it is in my very near future. In fact, I pray to God every day that He will not wait too long to take me home to be reunited with her.

I have no idea what a psychiatrist would say about that thought, but it comforts me to think that God might just be listening and be in a wish-granting frame of mind.

As for God, I am deeply disappointed in Him. I have only loved one woman throughout my entire adult life, and I have been completely faithful to her. Peggy is truly the only woman I have ever thought of spending my life with. Now it appears that God only intended for us to spend a lot of years together, not all of our lives.

I can't be mad at Him for that, but I can be enormously disappointed in Him, all the while accepting that it is His will, and I must find a way to live with it. I do know that the motive and purpose of the things God does are not always readily apparent to me. Nevertheless I have no other choice than to accept them as His will.

I can honestly admit that during the first three months after Peggy's death I wondered if God took her away from me as a form of punishment for something I either did or failed to do. I am smart enough to know that I am not the only one questioning God's motives and reckoning in our lives. It is logical to believe that many, if not most people suffering from a similar loss of a loved one, are going through similar lapses in their faith, and that's what these questions represent, a lapse in faith.

I believe God genuinely cares about my grieving. His ways are not our ways, but I know he cares greatly for me while I am suffering from a broken heart—even though He caused the broken heart. I can't explain how the same God who caused the pain by taking away the love of my life genuinely cares that I am suffering greatly, but I know He will eventually heal my broken heart and help me to find a way through this terrible ordeal.

Over the last two months I've received more than 80 sympathy cards from friends and family, as well as from people who love Peggy that I don't even know. I've also received a lot of personal telephone calls from neighbors and church friends of mine, and some from friends of Peggy's whom I don't know, who genuinely sound concerned about how well I am reacting to my loss.

It is comforting to know that so many people care about how well I am recovering from the unexpected loss of my wife. I say unexpected because I was still shocked that she actually died. Even when they took her to the hospice center I was sure she would be there for a week or two, instead of 28-hours.

The important thing now is for me to get back to my daily life. It is a very strange adjustment because after so many years with two of us in the house, it is a terribly awful adjustment to constantly come home to an empty house. Even when we were working on different sides of our house I could always hear and feel Peggy's presence and it was more than comforting to know that I could always count on having her near me.

She was a constant presence in our house, even when she was quiet in her office on the opposite side of the house from me, I could always feel her presence.

Over the years, we often took time out from out busy schedules to chat with each other during the day. One of us would invariably wonder down the hall and stop to chat no matter how busy we were. Peggy was always very engaging no matter our moods. And no matter how much busy work we had to do, we always spent the evenings together. Evenings were a special part of the day when we regularly enjoyed being together.

It is also a new experience to have to do all the things that I took for granted she would do. She was such a competent and energetic wife when it came to keeping up with our home that I took for granted much that she did. Now I appreciate more than ever all the things she took care of. She always insisted she wash and iron our clothes, even when I suggested we could afford to send them out. She just wouldn't have that! Now I wash my clothes every Sunday.

One thing I decided early on after her death was to not make any major decisions for at least a year. The thought of making a quick and stupid decision frightens me. Quite a few people have suggested that I sell our house and move into an apartment. There is simply no way I would even consider such a decision.

Even though there is a lot more room than I will ever need by myself, I have a lifetime of memories in our house, and there is no way I will give up those memories, not to mention all the mementos, furnishings, and decorations that were uniquely Peggy. Even though now many of them make me cry every time I look at them, I know that eventually they will be cherished memories of her.

All the people who have offered to help me also overwhelm me. They all want to do something to help me get through this period, but I tell them there is just not anything they or anyone else can do right now. My biggest chore right now is not work, either in the house or outside of the house. My biggest chore right now is to go day-to-day with a minimum of breakdowns.

Eventually I may need some help around the house, but for now I have a lady whom Peggy hired many years ago who comes every Thursday to clean. She has been helping us for so long that she is a very dear friend. She is an efficient and caring extension to our family that Peggy and I both cared deeply about, and I look forward to having her clean our house every week. That's the only help I need for now.

The biggest benefit at the moment is the wonderful support I get from friends. As I mentioned earlier, I have several close friends who I go to breakfast with every week. We've been doing that for a lot of years. They allow me to vent, cry, or do whatever I need to do to relieve the stress I feel. I'm sure they have no idea how much that helps me get through the weeks of grieving.

I find that even writing this imperfect piece of literature is a wonderful stress reducer. It helps me coalesce my thoughts and figure out how to react to them. It may not have occurred to you, but this is a huge new experience for me. I haven't had to think about how to live alone since I was in the Navy or in college, more than 65 years ago. To help me cope, I've been researching resources on the Internet that offer suggestions for how to handle grief, and I'm finding that there are also a lot of books on the topic.

I'm sure over the coming months I will find a lot of help from friends, neighbors, books, and Internet resources to help me weather this emotional storm. I recognize there is nothing new under the sun. Everything I am experiencing has already been addressed by lots of people over the years.

I have read a few pamphlets that suggest it is possible to forget details about the spouse you lost. I can assure you that will never be the case with me. I will stay connected to my memory of Peggy until we are reunited in Heaven. The reason I hurt so much right now is because I absolutely adored my wife for my entire adult life. In fact, I still do adore her and will continue to adore her for as long as I live.

There is no way that I will ever forget any of the details of our love affair over the years. I may forget about some of the details of things we did, but I will never forget the details of our love. In fact, I still haven't cleaned out her closet, dresser drawers, and cabinets. I figure I have plenty of time to do that, and I am in no hurry to clean out some of those memories.

I have had mixed recommendations from friends concerning when it would be best to go through my wife's possessions. Some folks think I should do it now, while others tell me to take my time. I find myself doing a bit of both. A nephew and his wife have taken some of Peggy's things, but there are still many things I will have to eventually move out of our house.

CHAPTER EIGHT

Other Possible Stages of Grief

While many researchers and authors agree with the legendary Elisabeh Kubler-Ross' five stages of grief, some authors and researchers believe there are more. I fell like I ought to mention them, but not spend a lot of time on them because some of the extra stages seem to me to be expansions of the previous five.

Recover-from-grief.com claims there are seven stages of grief. It acknowledges that they believe it is important to interpret the stages loosely, and expect much individual variation. For instance, following the death of a loved one, it states "it is actually normal and expected for you to be very depressed and sad eight months later."

As you might expect, some people think individuals should get over their grief much quicker so they can "rejoin the land of the living."

It lists its stages as:

- *Shock and Denial*. Similar to the first stage in Elisabeh Kubler-Rosses five stages.
- *Pain and Guilt*. It claims that as the shock wears off, it is replaced with the suffering of unbelievable pain, and that it is important that the surviving loved one experience the pain fully and not hide it, void it, or escape from it with alcohol or drugs.

- *Anger and Bargaining.* Also similar to stages two and three in Rosses five stages,.
- *Depression, Reflection, Loneliness.* Similar to stage four in Rosses five stages.
- *The Upward Turn.* As you start to adjust to life without your loved one, your life becomes a little calmer and more organized. Your physical symptoms lessen.
- *Reconstruction and Working Through.* As you become more functional, your mind starts working again, and you find yourself seeking realistic solutions to problems posed by life without your loved one.
- *Acceptance and Hope.* Similar to stage five in Rosses five stages.

Journey Through Grief.com lists the seven stages of grief in a slightly different scenario. It lists them as: 1) Shock, 2) Denial, 3) Anger, 4) Guilt, 5) Sorrow and Depression, 6) Acceptance, and 7) Engaging Life.

In **ARTICLE/.NET**, Marsha Johnson, writer, speaker, and author of **Emerald's Garden**, takes yet a different approach and lists eight stages of grief. Many are similar to the Five Stages of Grief and the Seven Stages of Grief, but use slightly different terms. Her stages are: 1) Shock, 2) Emotional Release, 3) Panic, 4) Guilt, 5) Hostility, 6) Inability to Resume Business-As-Usual, 7) Reconciliation of Grief, and 8) Hope.

In all of these various stages of grief, whether five, seven, or eight, all seem to agree that understanding the stages of grief provides reassurance that the wide range of emotions being experienced are common, normal, and not unusual.

A **WebMD** article, "What Is Normal Grieving, and What are the Stages of Grief," explains that grief is a natural response to losing someone or something that's important to you.

> "You may feel a variety of emotions, like sadness or loneliness. And you might experience it for a number of different reasons. Every person goes through these

phases in his or her own way. You may go back and forth between them, or skip one or more stages altogether. Reminders of your loss, like the anniversary of a death or a familiar song, can trigger the return of grief, even after months of feeling like you have fully recovered. Everyone grieves differently. But, if you understand your emotions, take care of yourself and seek support, you can heal."

CONCLUSIONS

It is absolutely necessary to understand that grief and depression are two distinctly different things. While grief can lead to depression, they are different and need to be understood separately. Grief is a natural and normal reaction to the loss of a loved one. Over time it will ebb and flow and, even after a lengthy period of months or years when you are functioning normally and least expect it, you can see something that reminds you of a special time that you and your spouse loved, and you can suddenly go into a deep funk for a few days.

However, major or clinical depression is a serious but treatable illness that usually requires medical attention from a professional, e.g., a family physician, psychiatrist, or psychologist. Serious depression can consume an individual. It can be constant, steady and unrelenting. The depressed person can begin to feel that he or she will never recover from the debilitating fog they must maneuver through every day.

The purpose of this book is not to focus on depression. That would be better left to a doctor to discuss. The point of this book is merely to record my wife's personal experiences with metastatic ovarian cancer and my personal experiences with grief. I don't have a medical background and do not pretend to know specifically how other people should or will react to situations that are the same or similar to our experiences with these dramatic issues. I can only relate how this period affected my wife and me.

Nevertheless, it seemed to me that it might be helpful for others who are going through similar ordeals to see how my wife and I were affected by her cancer and my grief. But everyone who reads this book must keep in mind that how we reacted to our stressful issues is unique and may not apply to the reader. Every reference source I've found on grief says the same thing: grief is very personal and unique to each individual.

My wife, Peggy, is the singularly most important and inspirational person I've ever known, especially when it comes to facing a terrible ordeal. She faced it with courage and faith in our Lord and his son, Jesus Christ. I have suffered a major heart attack and almost died three times, but it pales in contrast to what my wife went through over the 18-months she struggled with ovarian cancer.

While her cancer consumed her, I never once heard her complain about anything. She never once said "Why me God?" Even though I didn't believe her, she routinely said to me "I'm miserable, but I don't have any pain." I am convinced she said that because she didn't want me to worry about her. She was very concerned about how her failing health would affect me. Right up to the day she died, she assured me that even though she was miserable, she was not suffering any pain.

All the time she was being treated at the Cancer Care Center of Brevard, near Palm Bay, Florida, where she received an infusion of chemotherapy every three weeks, she never once complained to me, or to anyone else that I know of. Instead, she developed a platonic, but loving, relationship with her oncologist, Gregory B. Hoang, M.D., and the nurses who attended her throughout the year. In fact, after she died I received a sympathy card signed by everyone on the staff at the cancer center.

During her treatments, I was always concerned that it might have been better if we had gone to the Moffitt Cancer Center near Tampa, Florida. It has as its motto: A Lasting Commitment to the Prevention and Cure of Cancer, and it has a sterling reputation. It would have been worth the two-hour drive to be assured that she was getting the best possible treatment for her cancer. That is not to suggest that the Cancer Care Center of Brevard didn't provide outstanding treatments. It merely acknowledges that there were other options that we might have taken advantage of.

In fact, one of our neighbors, a very dear friend, was being treated at the Moffitt Cancer Center while Peggy was being treated at the Cancer Care Center of Brevard, and our neighbor was very pleased with the treatments she was receiving there. In fact, she is still being treated at the Moffitt Center.

I don't remember who recommended that Peggy go to the Cancer Care Center of Brevard, but once she was there, she was completely satisfied with the care she was receiving. Everyone on the staff treated her professionally and with lots of warmth. Peggy was completely happy with her cancer care.

Even so, I offered to take her to the Moffitt Cancer Center, but she declined. She was very pleased with her treatments at the Cancer Care Center generally, and was especially pleased with her oncologist. Dr. Hoang was and is one of the most compassionate and caring doctors we have ever seen. Peggy and I were both impressed with the quality of care he and his staff offered cancer patients. Dr. Hoang went well beyond minimal care while she was being treated.

He would call Peggy from his home in the evening and on the weekends to see how she was reacting to the chemotherapy. Every time we visited the center, he would make time to discuss her condition with both of us, answering our questions in layman terms so we could be sure to understand exactly what was happening during Peggy's treatments.

Even so, I still occasionally wonder if I made a mistake by not insisting my wonderful wife check out the Moffitt Center. I worried about it for quite a while, but Peggy assured me she was completely satisfied with the care she was getting from Dr. Hoang and the Cancer Center staff. Even though I worried about it from time to time, my concern was fleeting because I knew how she felt about the treatments she was receiving.

It was natural for me to questions my own judgments in retrospect because there was always a tinge of guilt, wondering if there was anything else I could have done to slow down the progress of the cancer or to help her in other ways.

What complicated our relationship was how reluctant she was to be a burden on me. I relished taking care of her and only wished I could do more. It crushed me to watch her suffer and to know there was simply nothing I could do to help her.

During the later stages of her cancer, she would not let anyone else help her. I think she just didn't want other people to see how much she had wasted away. At any rate, I relished the fact that she depended on me throughout her final stages of cancer. It created some images I would rather not have of her suffering, but those were unavoidable.

We would sit together for hours watching television programs we regularly enjoyed. However, all through this period I wondered how much time I had left to enjoy being with her. We both knew the end was near, but we didn't know how close it really was.

Not only that, we really didn't talk much about the approaching end to her ordeal. She was comfortable with it; I was not. The weaker she got and the more help she needed, the more I worried about the approaching reality of her passing.

I simply wasn't prepared for the sudden end, but I don't think I would have been ready if I had known six months in advance of a date certain that she would expire. I think what bothered me the most was how quickly she died after she decided to stop taking the chemotherapy.

Dr. Hoang had explained to us that Peggy's cancer was very aggressive and that without chemotherapy she would only have about two more months to live. He said with chemotherapy she might live another six months. I took him at his word because he has been treating cancer patients most of his life.

Peggy and I discussed the options. Knowing how miserable she was on chemotherapy, I blessed whatever she decided to do; all the while wanting her to do whatever would keep her alive the longest. I could not stand the thought of losing her.

Dr. Hoang wanted to try a new, more powerful chemotherapy, thinking it might prolong her life for a while. She decided to try one treatment of the new chemotherapy to see how well it worked, or more importantly, how miserable it made her feel. Well, she tried it and it made her undeniably miserable, so she decided to stop the chemotherapy, knowing full well the potential effect would be a shorter life expectancy.

While I recognize that doctors are not mini-gods and their estimates are just that, I was aghast at how fast the end time came when she decided to quit chemotherapy. Dr. Hoang had predicted that without chemotherapy she would have about two months to live. Boy, was he off by a lot.

Her condition worsened rapidly. She refused to eat, although I occasionally got her to sip a protein drink, and her weigh loss quickened to the point that by the time she died she had lost 80 pounds. She got so weak she could not even get out of her chair. Fortunately, her chair is a recliner that folds back to the point it virtually became a bed. She stayed in her chair for the last two weeks of her life, with me picking her up and taking her to the bathroom when needed.

Even though she was not strong enough to get out of her chair, she maintained her sense of humor, was animated and kept a running conversation with me, while we watched television. I wanted so much more time with her. But it wasn't to be! When she got to the Hospice Center and they gave her morphine and a sedative, she was gone in 28 hours.

That was a shock to me because before they would let her come to the center she was interviewed at home by a professional, who let us know that no one could stay at the hospice center for more than two weeks. If a patient survived more than two weeks, the patient had to go home and wait until he or she was closer to the end. That suggested to us that they thought she might last more than two weeks.

I don't suppose it matters much to anyone else, but I was not prepared to lose her in only 28 hours. I fully expected that she would be there for at least a week or so. In retrospect, that wouldn't have mattered. I'm sure I would have been just as shocked and disappointed at the end of two weeks.

We had several years ago arranged for our end times with the Ammen Cremation and Funeral Care Center, in Melbourne, Florida. We both elected to be cremated and selected two beautiful matching urns for our ashes. We also paid in advance for our cremation services and shipment of our ashes to Arlington National Cemetery.

Knowing she was no longer in the shell of her body, but was in the arms of our Lord, I elected to not watch her cremation. When she died I had her body shipped to the Ammen Family Cremation and Funeral Care Center where she was cremated and her ashes were placed in the beautiful urn we had previously selected.

The folks at the Ammen center were considerate, professional, and caring. They treated me with the utmost respect and kindness. I would recommend them to anyone who has a death in their family.

I will keep Peggy's urn at home until I die, at which point I will be cremated and my ashes will be placed in an urn that matches the one holding her ashes.

At that point the Ammen Family Cremation and Funeral Care Center will ship both of our urns to the Arlington National Cemetery to be placed together in Arlington's crematorium where we will reside for as long as there is an Arlington National Cemetery.

Now I have gone through most of the five major stages of grief and am finally moving on with my life, which is certainly what Peggy would have wanted me to do. I have returned to serving as an usher at church and was pleasantly surprised to have so many Christian friends rush up to welcome me back and let me know how much I was missed. My neighbors have been wonderful, providing food and encouragement.

All in all, I feel like I am on the road to recovery, although I still have a great deal of trouble speaking about my wife when folks who don't know she died ask about her. I still cry frequently and often at unexpected times. At night I have a difficult time going to sleep, because my mind drifts back to my life with Peggy. Once I get to sleep I sleep well, but I have trouble getting to sleep. A few times it has taken me several hours to fall asleep, so I got a prescription from my family doctor for sleeping pills that help.

I also still have a lot of trouble looking at pictures of her, although I have them hanging all over my office. Those pictures just make me wish she were still here. I know that eventually I will cherish all of the pictures I have of us together, but for now they are sometimes very painful to look at.

I am emerging out of my shell and re-engaging with the world, which is good, but I still pray every day that God will not wait too long to take me home to be with her. My ultimate goal is still to be reunited with my sweet Peggy.

We use to go to movies a couple of times a month, but I quit going to movies about six months before she died, and haven't returned to see one yet. But I plan to go to a movie soon to see something that I think we would both enjoy.

I have placed her urn on our fireplace mantel, and I talk to her every time I walk past the urn. I doubt she can hear me, but it comforts me to talk to her, just as it comforts me to talk to my God. My life has changed dramatically, and it will undoubtedly take a long time to adjust to the new normal, but I will survive until God takes me home to be with Peggy.

I have been amazed at how many people have warned me against committing suicide, but that was completely unnecessary. From the time I was a young altar boy in the Roman Catholic Church until now that I am an Evangelical Protestant, I have acknowledged that God alone determines the time for birth and death. And he takes very seriously anyone who invades His domain by committing suicide.

As I recall, in the Roman Catholic Church suicide is considered to be an unforgivable mortal sin that will condemn an individual to hell, because there is no way for the person committing suicide to repent for that serious sin.

For centuries, the official stance of the Catholic Church prohibited funerals and burials of individuals who committed suicide. Catholics were generally denied funerals as a means of discouraging the act of suicide. In recent years, however, the Church has reversed its prohibition and has taken a more lenient view on suicide.

All Christians are taught that at the time of death God immediately judges each of us, and He decides where we will spend eternity. Even Protestants believe that suicide is a serious offense against God that can have terrible consequences.

My history in both the Catholic and Protestant churches gives me enough caution to serve as a deterrent to taking such a risk with God. I would never do anything that could cause me to be permanently separated from my wife for all of eternity. That is simply a non-starter.

In my belief system, God alone must determine when we die, and it is always supposed to be in His time. I have no choice but to wait patiently for God to decide when He wants me to be reunited with Peggy in heaven.

Meanwhile, I have great friends who look after me and keep me on a stable plane. Two of those close friends and I go to breakfast every week to discuss the world's problems and to offer our unbiased suggestions for solving them. One friend is not even a Christian, but he is tolerant, loving, and extremely considerate of my religious beliefs.

It is my close friends, like these two, who will get me through the coming years while I wait to join Peggy. In the meantime, I have restarted my daily walks. I now walk two miles most days. That is an age limitation. For many years Peggy and I were long-distance runners. We would run eight miles almost every day and 10 or 15 miles on Saturday or Sunday.

Peggy stopped running long before I did. When we were in our forties we entered a race at the Naval Academy in Maryland. It was advertised as a course of gently rolling hills. Turned out the hills were a lot more up and down than rolling. Those hills caused Peggy so much pain that when we got home she announced that she was finished with running. She was serious and never ran again!

I continued running until I turned 65, when I gave up running and racquetball. I forgot to mention that I also played racquetball about four times a week. The running and racquetball eventually took a toll on my back and knees, so I gave them up and took up walking a few miles a day instead.

Eventually, as I approached age 80, I gave up waking so much too. But, since I've lost Peggy I have taken up walking again. Until I get my legs back in shape, I'm limited to about two miles each day. Eventually, I will return to walking five miles each day.

The benefit is that it keeps my mind occupied and takes up a lot of time. I use to run seven or eight minute miles. Now I walk twenty-minute miles. I say goodbye to Peggy before I leave the house and when I return I yell, "I'm back" as soon as I come into the house. I know it's silly, but it's comforting for me to continue talking to her.

I am very grateful that God allowed me to get through the grieving process without becoming clinically depressed. My depressive moods were short and not intense, allowing me to move on with my life.

I know that I will still have periods of grief and moments of depression, particularly whenever I have to talk about her, but those distractions are fewer and much further apart now.

People constantly give me well-intentioned advice, some of it quite good and some of it not so good, but I take their advice "with a grain of salt." While I'm on the road to recovery, I still keep Peggy foremost in my thoughts, because I'm in a permanent state of waiting to be reunited with my sweet wonderful wife! My ultimate goal is to spend eternity with her in heaven! I pray every day that the wait will not be too long, even though my friends caution me to quit thinking like that. At this point in my life reuniting with Peggy is my one consistent long-term goal.

However, in the short term I have adopted a two-year-old Domestic Short Hair, male, black and white cat. He has adapted to me well and provides company. He sometimes takes my mind off of my sweet, wonderful Peggy.

He is full of energy and has unintentionally destroyed a lot of stuff around the house. He doesn't mean to do that, but he is full of energy, climbs up on furniture and bumps into things-knocking them off to break. It is a small price to pay for not being so lonely.

EDITOR'S NOTE

Don is retired and lives in Melbourne, Florida, where he continues writing occasional articles on topics of interest. He has close friends in his neighborhood and at his church, all of who provide wonderful support as he learns to live without Peggy.

www.ingramcontent.com/pod-product-compliance
Lightning Source LLC
Chambersburg PA
CBHW021451070526
44577CB00002B/360